WESTMINSTER PUBLIC LIBRARY

3 3020 01118 0386

CH

S0-AKZ-870

Westminster Public Library
3705 W 112th Ave
Westminster, CO 80031
www.westminsterlibrary.org

PLUTO

GOD OF THE UNDERWORLD

by Teri Temple and Emily Temple
Illustrated by Eric Young

Gods and
Goddesses
of Ancient
Rome

MEDIA ENHANCED BOOKS
AV²
BY WEIGL™
ADDED VALUE · AUDIO VISUAL

www.av2books.com

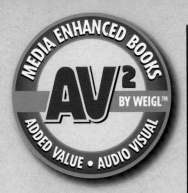

AV² provides enriched content that supplements and complements this book. Weigl's AV² books strive to create inspired learning and engage young minds in a total learning experience.

Your AV² Media Enhanced books come alive with...

Audio
Listen to sections of the book read aloud.

Key Words
Study vocabulary, and complete a matching word activity.

Video
Watch informative video clips.

Quizzes
Test your knowledge.

Go to **www.av2books.com,** and enter this book's unique code.

BOOK CODE

AVZ29335

Embedded Weblinks
Gain additional information for research.

Slide Show
View images and captions, and prepare a presentation.

AV² by Weigl brings you media enhanced books that support active learning.

Try This!
Complete activities and hands-on experiments.

... and much, much more!

Published by AV² by Weigl
350 5th Avenue, 59th Floor
New York, NY 10118
Website: www.av2books.com

Printed in Brainerd, Minnesota, United States
1 2 3 4 5 6 7 8 9 0 22 21 20 19 18

102018
102318

Project Coordinator: Jared Siemens
Art Director: Terry Paulhus

Copyright © 2020 AV² by Weigl
All rights reserved. No part of this publication may be reproduced, stored in a retrieval system, or transmitted in any form or by any means, electronic, mechanical, photocopying, recording, or otherwise, without the prior written permission of the publisher.

Library of Congress Control Number: 2018961496

ISBN 978-1-4896-9511-6 (hardcover)
ISBN 978-1-4896-9512-3 (softcover)
ISBN 978-1-4896-9513-0 (multi-user eBook)

Every reasonable effort has been made to trace ownership and to obtain permission to reprint copyright material. The publishers would be pleased to have any errors or omissions brought to their attention so that they may be corrected in subsequent printings.

Weigl acknowledges Getty Images, Alamy, and Shutterstock as its primary image suppliers for this title.

CONTENTS

INTRODUCTION

In **ancient** times, Romans believed in spirits or gods called *numina*. In Latin, numina means "divine will" or "power." The Romans took part in religious rituals to please the gods. They felt the gods had powers that could make their lives better.

As the Roman government grew more powerful, its armies **conquered** many neighboring lands. Romans often adopted beliefs from these new cultures. They greatly admired the Greek arts and sciences. Gradually, the Romans combined the Greek myths and religion with their own. These stories shaped and influenced each part of a Roman citizen's daily life. Ancient Roman poets, such as Ovid and Virgil, wrote down these tales of wonder. Their writings became a part of Rome's great history. To the Romans, however, these stories were not just for entertainment. Roman mythology was their key to understanding the world.

ANCIENT ROMAN SOCIETIES

Ancient Roman society was divided into several groups. The patricians were the most powerful and wealthy group. They often owned land and held power in the government. The plebeians worked for the patricians. Slaves were prisoners of war or children without parents. Some slaves were freed and enjoyed most of the rights of citizens.

CHARACTERS AND PLACES

ANCIENT ROME

Adriatic Sea

N

W

E

S

• ROME

**Olympian Gods
(uh-LIM-pee-uhn / GAHDZ)**
Ceres with daughter Proserpine, Mercury,
Vulcan, Venus with son Cupid, Mars,
Juno, Jupiter, Neptune, Minerva, Apollo,
Diana, Bacchus, Vesta, and Pluto

Titans (TIE-tinz)
The 12 children of Terra and Caelus;
godlike giants who are said to
represent the forces of nature

Tyrrhenian Sea

Underworld (UHN-der-wurld)
The land of the dead; ruled over by
the god of the dead, Pluto; must cross
the River Styx to gain entrance

CERBERUS (SUR-bur-uhs)
Giant three-headed dog that guards
the entrance to the underworld

CERES (SEER-eez)
Goddess of the harvest;
mother of Proserpine

CYCLOPES (SIGH-clops)
One-eyed giants; children
of Terra and Caelus

**HECATONCHEIRES
(hek-a-TON-kear-eez)**
Monstrous creatures with 100 arms and
50 heads; children of Terra and Caelus

OPS (AHPS)
A Titaness; married to her brother, Saturn;
mother to the first six Olympian gods: Jupiter,
Neptune, Pluto, Juno, Vesta, and Ceres

ORPHEUS (OHR-fee-uhs)
Mortal who traveled to the underworld
to rescue his wife, Eurydice

PIRITHOUS (py-RITH-oh-uhs)
Tried to kidnap Proserpine and ended
up trapped in the underworld by Hades

PLUTO (PLOO-toh)
God of the underworld and death; son of
Saturn and Ops, married to Proserpine

PROSERPINE (PRAW-sur-pine)
Daughter of the goddess, Ceres; married to Pluto

SISYPHUS (SIS-i-fuhs)
Mortal whose punishment in the underworld
was to forever push a boulder up a hill

VENUS (VEE-nuhs)
Goddess of love and beauty; born of the sea
foam; wife of Vulcan; mother of Cupid

THE GOD OF THE UNDERWORLD

Pluto would become the god of death and lord of the underworld. Yet Pluto did not get off to a good start.

According to Roman mythology, there was only darkness at the beginning of time. Out of the darkness arose Mother Earth. She was also called Terra. She created the **heavens** and the god of the sky, called Caelus. Together, Terra and Caelus became the parents of a strong race of giants known as the Titans. The Titans represented the forces of nature. Without the Titans, there would be no stories of the Olympian gods.

Saturn, the youngest Titan, challenged his father, Caelus, to become ruler of the universe. The Titan fought his father in battle. Saturn won.

Saturn and his wife Ops went on to give birth to the first Olympian gods. But Saturn was nervous his children would defeat him, as he had defeated his own father. To protect himself, he swallowed each child after it was born. Ops was sad without her children. She devised a plan to set them free. After giving birth to their sixth child, she hid him on an island. She gave Saturn a wrapped stone, pretending it was their child, Jupiter.

When Jupiter was grown, he returned to his parents with a potion for Saturn. It made Saturn throw up his first five children and the stone. Three sisters, Vesta, Ceres, Juno, and two brothers, Neptune and Pluto, emerged from his stomach. The six Olympian gods were free.

The Olympian gods wanted to defeat Saturn, but they needed help. Saturn had imprisoned his other children, the **Cyclopes** and the **Hecatoncheires**, in the underworld. Jupiter released them. These creatures would help the gods.

The Hecatoncheires were fearsome warriors. The Cyclopes built weapons. They were skilled blacksmiths. They made Pluto a helmet of darkness. This helmet allowed him to move invisibly among his enemies.

The battle between the Titans and the gods lasted ten years. Eventually the gods had the advantage. Pluto used his helmet to sneak into the Titans' camp. He stole all of their weapons. Then, Jupiter blasted the Titans with a thunderbolt. The Cyclopes and Hecatoncheires threw boulders at the Titans.

The universe was nearly destroyed, so the Titans gave up. The world was finally at peace. After winning the battle, the Olympian gods built a new home on Mount Olympus. Now Jupiter was ruler. He divided the universe among his brothers. It was decided that Jupiter would be king of the gods and rule over the heavens. Neptune was made god of the seas. Pluto was granted reign over the underworld.

The Tennessee Titans of the National Football League (NFL) took their name from the Titans of Roman and Greek mythology. In 2017, the team scored 33 touchdowns.

Ancient Romans thought the underworld lay deep beneath the secret places of the earth. Both ancient Greeks and Romans thought some of the afterlife was desolate and unhappy. As a result, the underworld was a dark and miserable place, but it suited Pluto perfectly.

In the underworld, Pluto lived in a palace. Only the spirits knew what the palace looked like. It was crowded with the souls of the dead and locked with a heavy gate. Cold meadows surrounded Pluto's home. The meadows were filled with strange pale flowers called asphodel.

Pluto's appearance matched his lonely home. Pluto was majestic, yet **somber**. He always carried a scepter to show he protected the underworld. Pluto was a stern god. Prayer and sacrifice had no effect on him. Pluto was at home in the underworld, so he left the ruling of the universe and its problems to his siblings. He was not welcome on Earth or on Mount Olympus.

THE RIVERS OF THE UNDERWORLD

Five rivers surrounded the underworld. The only poet who wrote clearly about the geography of the underworld was Virgil. He said a path led to where the Archeron River joined the Cocytus River. Three more rivers separated the underworld from Earth. These rivers were called the Phlegethon, the Lethe, and the River Styx.

Though Pluto was a **grim** and somber god, he ruled the underworld well. He gave responsibilities to other beings. He also made sure everyone did his or her job correctly. When a person died, his or her spirit traveled to the underworld for judgment. The journey to the underworld was not easy. First, the spirits had to cross the River Styx. They paid the ferryman, Charon, a coin for passage to the underworld. The spirits had to row themselves across the river. Charon steered the boat.

Once across, the spirits passed Cerberus. He was a three-headed, dragon-tailed dog that guarded the underworld entrance. Cerberus did not bother the spirits. His job was to keep out the living. After passing Cerberus, the spirits reached a fork in the road. This was where they learned their fate. The three Judges of the Dead decided in which level of the underworld the spirit would live for eternity. Pluto did not help make these decisions.

JUDGES OF THE DEAD

The three judges that decided the fate of the dead were Rhadamanthus, Aeacus, and Minos. These judges were sons of Jupiter. They were given immortality and positions as judges as reward for creating law on Earth. Rhadamanthus was judge of the men from Asia. Aeacus was guardian of the keys of the underworld. He was also judge of the men from Europe. Minos was the final vote. Some myths say there was a fourth judge named Triptolemus.

The underworld had many different names in Roman mythology. These included Tartarus, Erebus, and Hades. Erebus was where the dead went first after they died. Tartarus was a deeper level. It was the prison of the Titans. The underworld was often incorrectly called Hades. This was actually the name of a Greek god.

Pluto watched his helpers carefully. He wanted the underworld to work smoothly. The Judges of the Dead decided which level a spirit lived in. The first level was reserved for spirits of heroes. Spirits lived here forever in paradise. Tartarus was home to the evildoers. Only the very wicked were sent to this level deep beneath the earth. Pluto sent the Furies to Tartarus to punish these souls. Most common souls went to a dull and dreary middle ground called Asphodel Meadows.

THE FURIES

The Furies were serpent-haired daughters of Terra. They lived in the underworld, where they served as goddesses of revenge. Pluto had the Furies punish people. The Furies traveled to Earth to find mortals who had committed terrible crimes. They especially despised murderers. The Furies punished the wicked by driving them to madness.

Pluto wanted a bride to help him rule his kingdom. Even though the underworld was full of spirits and Pluto's attendants, the god was still lonely. Venus, the goddess of love, wanted him to find love as well. She told her son, Cupid, to shoot Pluto with an arrow to make him fall in love.

Pluto's sister, Ceres, had a daughter named Proserpine. She grew up on Mount Olympus. Several of the gods wanted to marry her because she was very beautiful. Even Pluto took notice. With the help of Cupid's arrow, Pluto fell in love with Proserpine. He wanted her as his bride. But Pluto knew Ceres would never let Proserpine go to the underworld. So Pluto crafted a plan to carry her off.

Proserpine was playing with water **nymphs** in a fountain in Sicily, Italy, near Mount Etna, a volcano. She set off to pick flowers in a nearby meadow. A dark chariot pulled by black horses charged out of the volcano. Pluto was holding the reins. He took Proserpine by surprise and dragged her screaming into the underworld.

Mount Etna is the largest active volcano in Europe. The last major eruption was in 1992, but the volcano has almost continuous smaller eruptions.

When she discovered Proserpine was gone, Ceres was heartbroken. She wandered Earth in search of her beloved daughter. Ceres was the goddess of the harvest. She refused to let anything grow until she was reunited with her daughter. But Pluto refused to return Proserpine to Earth.

Ceres was so desperate she asked Jupiter for help. Jupiter knew he needed to fix the problem so plants would grow again. He sent Mercury to the underworld. Mercury was Jupiter's messenger. He found Proserpine in Pluto's gloomy palace. She was silent and somber, just like the god of the underworld. But when Proserpine saw Mercury she leapt to her feet. She was filled with hope that she would be reunited with her mother.

Pluto knew he had to follow Jupiter's command to send Proserpine back to Earth. Pluto offered Proserpine all the jewels and riches of Earth. He hoped to convince Proserpine to stay, but it did not work. To make sure she would remain, Pluto tricked her into eating a single pomegranate seed. According to the laws of the Fates, anyone who ate food of the underworld could never permanently return to the land of the living. The Fates were three of Jupiter's daughters. These goddesses spun and cut the threads of life. This meant the Fates determined a person's path.

Even though Jupiter was ruler of the universe, he also had to follow the laws of the Fates. Jupiter, however, managed to work out a deal with the Fates. Proserpine was allowed to leave the underworld to spend four months on Earth with her mother. During that time, Ceres provided plenty of crops for the humans on Earth.

The other eight months Proserpine spent with Pluto in the underworld. She ruled with Pluto as the queen of the underworld. But Proserpine was not happy. Neither was her mother. Ceres's grief brought winter during the time Proserpine was not with her. Earth was barren and cold.

The rulings of the Fates were final. Humans were forced to patiently wait for spring each year. Proserpine's return brought about the springtime. By allowing Proserpine time with her mother, Pluto assured a harvest for the people of Earth. Because of this, Pluto came to be known as the god of Earth's **fruitfulness**, not just death.

In the Roman calendar, the first day of spring begins March 25th. Winter begins December 25th.

Pluto was busy in the underworld with all of the problems death created. He worked all day and all night. Theseus and his friend Pirithous were two of the troublemakers Pluto had to deal with.

Pluto met Theseus and Pirithous when they traveled to the underworld to capture Proserpine. Pirithous wanted to marry the queen of the underworld. Theseus was helping to return a favor. They made their way to the underworld. They even got past Cerberus.

The two mortals arrived in Pluto's palace and informed him they had come for Proserpine. Pluto laughed, amused by their bravery. He invited them to take a seat and discuss their plan, but he never intended to let them succeed.

When they sat down, Theseus and Pirithous were suddenly unable to move or think. Pluto had tricked them into sitting in the Chairs of Forgetfulness. Their minds blank, the two remained stuck there for many years.

THESEUS

Theseus was a famous Greek hero from Athens. He was the son of Aegeus, king of Athens. Some myths say Theseus was the son of Neptune. Theseus played a role in many myths. He sailed with Jason and the Argonauts. He killed the Minotaur in the labyrinth on Crete. Theseus also kidnapped Helen from the Trojan War. And he was trapped in the underworld until Hercules set him free. Theseus continued to have adventures until his death.

The Greek hero Hercules encountered Theseus and Pirithous while he was trying to complete one of his 12 labors. Hercules traveled to the underworld to convince Pluto to let him borrow Cerberus. Hercules was able to free Theseus but not Pirithous. Pluto would not let him take the man who had tried to kidnap his wife. Pirithous was forced to spend eternity in the underworld.

Another story follows Orpheus and his beloved wife, Eurydice. When Eurydice died from a snakebite, Orpheus was sad. He thought he could not live without her. He traveled to the underworld to win her back. Orpheus charmed his way into the underworld by using his musical talents. Once there, Proserpine allowed Orpheus and Eurydice to leave. Pluto had one rule, though. Orpheus could not look back at Eurydice until they were safely past the borders of the underworld.

Orpheus agreed. But as they neared the edge of the underworld, he turned to check on his wife. As soon as he looked back, Eurydice was whisked back to the underworld. Orpheus had to spend the rest of his life alone.

The name Pluto comes from the Greek word *ploutos*, which means wealth. The ancient Romans originally worshiped him as the god of all metals, jewels, and riches that lie under the earth. Pluto was considered similar to the Greek god of the underworld, Hades, and the Roman god Dis Pater.

Pluto ruled over all of the regions of the dead. Pluto never personally punished or tortured those found guilty of evildoing. He watched over the decisions made by the three Judges. Pluto was the god of the dead, not the god of death. That privilege belonged to the Roman god Orcus.

Ancient Romans were convinced that just saying Pluto's name would attract his attention. The Romans did not know what Pluto would or would not do. During the festivals of the winter, animal sacrifices were made at the Roman Colosseum. In the middle of the arena, a fire was kept burning for sacrifices of animals with black fur. Pluto was also honored at funeral ceremonies. Slaves and servants dressed as Pluto or his ferryman, Charon.

Pluto was not considered one of the 12 major gods in the Roman Pantheon, but he still played an important role in the cycle of life. There would always be a need for the god of the dead.

DIS PATER AND PLUTO

Dis Pater was the Romans' original god of the underworld. In Latin, his name meant "rich father." Dis Pater was god of riches, fertile land, and mineral wealth from underground. Later, he was combined with the deities Pluto and Orcus. The ancient Roman people feared Dis Pater.

PRINCIPAL GODS OF ROMAN MYTHOLOGY— A FAMILY TREE

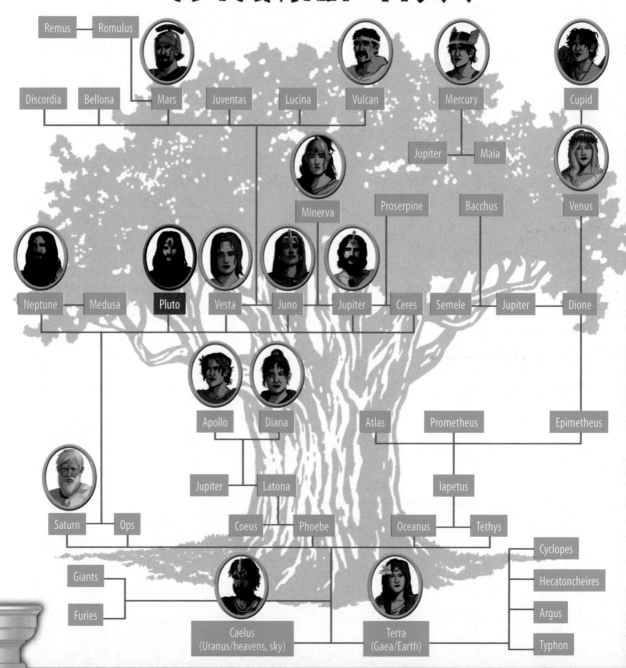

Remus — Romulus

Discordia — Bellona — Mars — Juventas — Lucina — Vulcan — Mercury — Cupid

Jupiter — Maia

Minerva — Proserpine — Bacchus — Venus

Neptune — Medusa — Pluto — Vesta — Juno — Jupiter — Ceres — Semele — Jupiter — Dione

Apollo — Diana — Atlas — Prometheus — Epimetheus

Saturn — Ops — Jupiter — Latona — Iapetus

Coeus — Phoebe — Oceanus — Tethys

Giants — Cyclopes

Furies — Hecatoncheires

Argus

Caelus (Uranus/heavens, sky) — Terra (Gaea/Earth) — Typhon

KEY WORDS

ancient: from the very distant past

conquered: to take control through military force

Cyclopes: one-eyed giants

fruitfulness: when something is productive

grim: uninviting and lacking a sense of humor

heavens: the sky, where the sun, moon, stars, and planets are located

Hecatoncheires: a creature with 50 heads and 100 arms

mortal: a human being who can die

nymphs: spirits that are believed to live in rivers, forests, or other natural places

somber: serious and at times negative in mood

INDEX

Log on to www.av2books.com

AV² by Weigl brings you media enhanced books that support active learning. Go to www.av2books.com, and enter the special code found on page 2 of this book. You will gain access to enriched and enhanced content that supplements and complements this book. Content includes video, audio, weblinks, quizzes, a slide show, and activities.

AV² Online Navigation

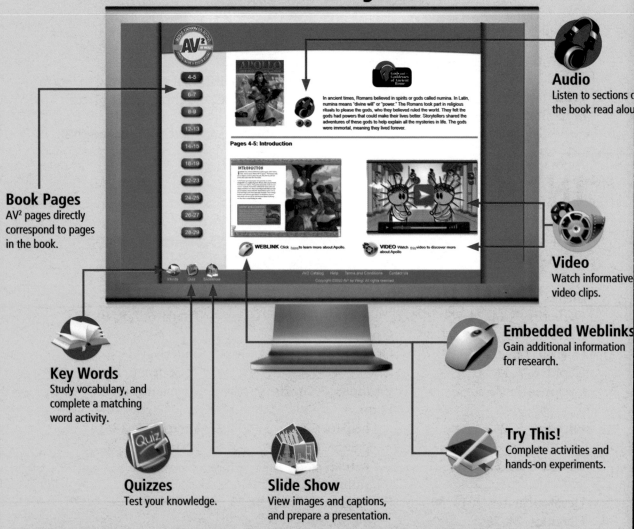

Book Pages
AV² pages directly correspond to pages in the book.

Audio
Listen to sections of the book read aloud.

Video
Watch informative video clips.

Key Words
Study vocabulary, and complete a matching word activity.

Embedded Weblinks
Gain additional information for research.

Quizzes
Test your knowledge.

Slide Show
View images and captions, and prepare a presentation.

Try This!
Complete activities and hands-on experiments.

AV² was built to bridge the gap between print and digital. We encourage you to tell us what you like and what you want to see in the future.

Sign up to be an AV² Ambassador at www.av2books.com/ambassador.

Due to the dynamic nature of the Internet, some of the URLs and activities provided as part of AV² by Weigl may have changed or ceased to exist. AV² by Weigl accepts no responsibility for any such changes. All media enhanced books are regularly monitored to update addresses and sites in a timely manner. Contact AV² by Weigl at 1-866-649-3445 or av2books@weigl.com with any questions, comments, or feedback.